Let's
Knit

DK | Penguin Random House

Senior designer **Hannah Moore**
Project editor **Anne Hildyard**
Photographer **Andy Crawford**
Senior producer **Ché Creasey**
Producer, Pre-Production **Dragana Puvacic**
Jacket designer **Amy Keast**
Creative technical support **Sonia Charbonnier**
Managing editor **Penny Smith**
Managing art editor **Marianne Markham**
Art director **Jane Bull**
Publisher **Mary Ling**

First published in Great Britain in 2015 by
Dorling Kindersley Limited
80 Strand, London WC2R 0RL

A CIP catalogue record for this book
is available from the British Library.
ISBN: 978–0–2411–9723–3

Printed in China.
All images © Dorling Kindersley Limited
For further information see: www.dkimages.com

A WORLD OF IDEAS
SEE ALL THERE IS TO KNOW
www.dk.com

Make lovely knitted things.

Contents

Learn how to knit.

Introduction

To start knitting you need yarn and needles. Then you learn how to hold the needles, make a slip knot, cast on, do knit stitch, and purl stitch. In no time at all, you'll be knitting. Don't worry about making mistakes, everyone drops stitches to begin with. With practice, it will come right. Then, you can go on to make some of the adorable projects in the book.

Getting started

At the beginning of each project is a panel listing what **you will need**. Then, with the help of an adult, gather together an essential knitting kit (see pages 6–7), and start knitting!

Have a go, we're really easy to knit

Safety

All the projects in this book are to be made under adult supervision. Always take extra care when sharp implements such as knitting needles, scissors, sewing needles, or pins are used to make a project. **Ask an adult to help you.**

Remember to take care with sharp objects.

Don't be a knitwit, keep safe when you knit.

Knitting kit

Here are the things you need to make all the **projects** in this book.

Double knit yarn

Knitting needles

Crochet hook

Coloured felt

Bet you can't wait to make something!

Chunky yarn

Yarn

You'll need double knit yarn for most of the projects in the book.

Tape measure

Knitting needles

You'll need 4mm (No 6) knitting needles for most of the projects.

Decorations

Buttons, beads, sequins, and googly eyes

Sewing needles

Needle threader (optional)

Thimble

Embroidery threads

Sewing thread

Scissors

Pincushion with pins

Ribbons

Selection of buttons for eyes and decorations

Make a slip knot

To start knitting, first you need yarn and needles.
The next step is to make a **slip knot**.

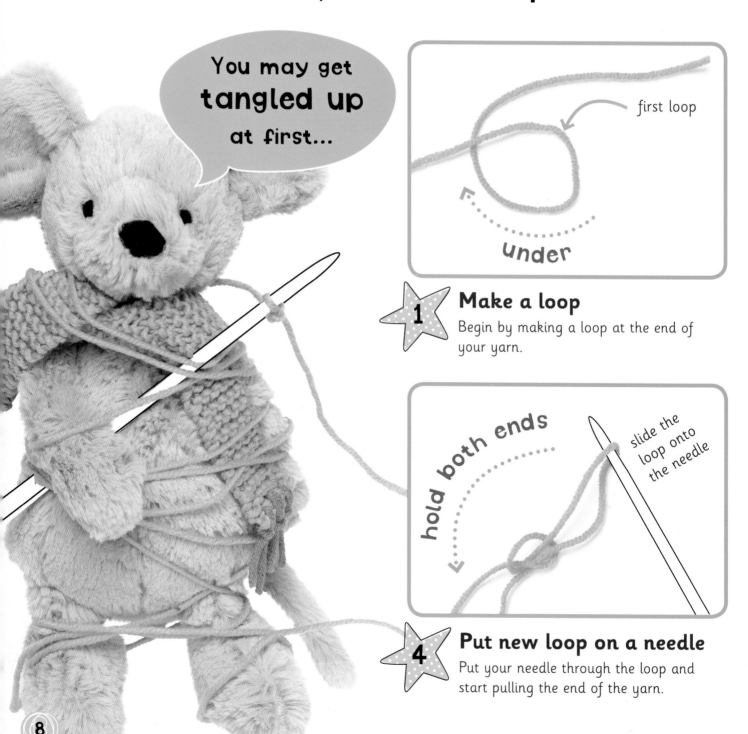

You may get **tangled up** at first...

first loop

under

1 Make a loop
Begin by making a loop at the end of your yarn.

hold **both ends**

slide the loop onto the needle

4 Put new loop on a needle
Put your needle through the loop and start pulling the end of the yarn.

This will become your **first** **stitch**

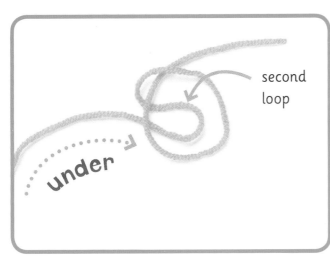

second loop

under

pull through

2 **Make a new loop**
Bring the yarn through the first loop to make a new loop.

3 **Pull the new loop through**
Keep pulling the new loop until it is big enough for your needle to go through.

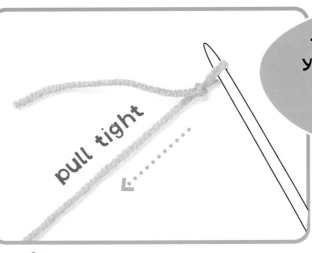

pull tight

... but with practice you'll be able to make **a perfect slip knot!**

5 **Pull the end tight**
Keep pulling the yarn until the loop is tight enough to stay on the needle.

Casting on

You've already made your first stitch with your slip knot. Now add as many stitches as you like – then you can start knitting.

hold the yarn in your **left hand**

make a **loop** on your thumb

1

Slip knot on the needle
Before you add any stitches, start with a slip knot on your needle. It's knotted so that it stays on the needle.

2

Wrap yarn around thumb
To start making a new stitch, hold the needle in one hand, then wrap the yarn around the front of the thumb.

Now you're **ready** to **start**

Count your stitches **one, two, three...**

1 2 3 4 5 6

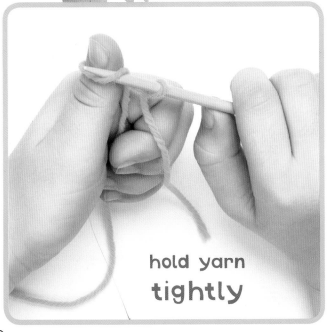

hold yarn **tightly**

now you have cast on **two stitches**

3 ### Slip needle into the loop

Put your needle through the loop on your thumb. Gently lift the yarn off your thumb so the loop slips onto the needle.

4 ### Pull the yarn tight

Pull the yarn tight so the loop sits next to the first one you made with the slip knot. Keep going until you have all the stitches you need.

knitting!

Knit stitch

Percy penguin has knitted a few rows to start you off. Knit stitch is used in all the projects, and it's easy to learn.

into the loop

wind the yarn firmly around your fingers

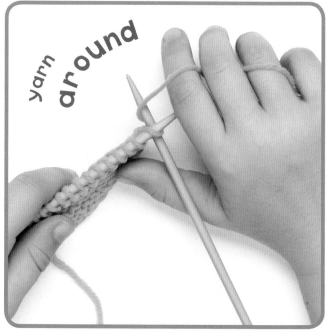

yarn around

1

Start with the first stitch
Push the end of the needle into the front of the first stitch.

2

Wrap yarn around needle
Bring the yarn under and around the needle so the yarn is between the two needles.

When you finish a row swap the needles

All the stitches are on your **right needle.**

See how many rows I've done!

When you knit every row in knit stitch, the pattern you make is called **garter stitch**.

pull loop **through**

take loop **off**

3 Draw yarn through stitch
Bring the right needle with the yarn through the loop on the left needle.

4 Slip stitch off the needle
Gently slip the new loop, and stitch, off the left needle, onto the right needle.

round in your hands and start another row.

Now, swap the needle to your **left hand.**

Casting off

When your knitting is the length you want it, it's time to **cast off**. This means leaving a neat edge.

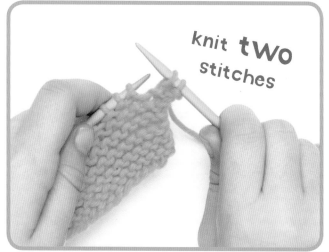

knit **two** stitches

 1 **Knit two stitches**
Knit the first two stitches from the left needle onto the right needle.

pick up the first **stitch**

 2 **Pick up the first stitch**
Push the left needle into the first stitch on the right needle and pick it up.

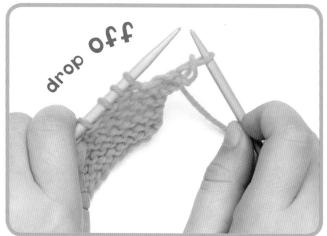

drop **off**

 4 **Drop the first stitch**
Let the first stitch drop off the needle. Knit another stitch, then repeat steps 2–4.

make a **loop**

 5 **At the last stitch**
With your needle, open out the last stitch to make a big loop.

Sew in the ends

Thread the loose yarn onto a needle and sew down the edge of the knitting.

Pull the needle and yarn through.

lift the stitch over

Cut the yarn close to the knitting.

3

Lift the first stitch over

Carefully carry the first stitch over the second stitch.

The neatened edge looks like this.

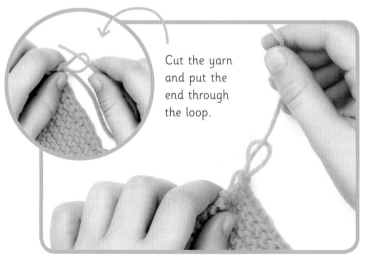

Cut the yarn and put the end through the loop.

6

Pull yarn through loop

Push the end of the yarn all the way through, and pull tight.

Now you've learned to knit, why not make a cool scarf like mine?

Get stripy

Stripes are fun. You can use lots of lovely colours, and make thin or fat **stripes,** or a mixture of both.

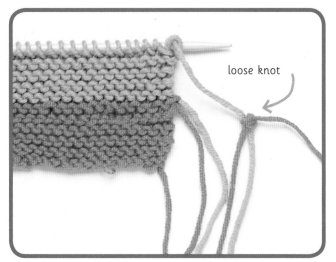

loose knot

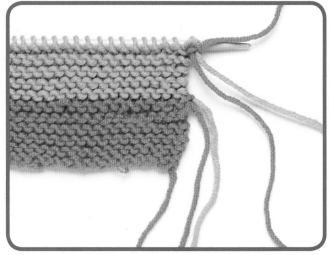

1 **Joining a new colour**
Tie the new yarn to the first one with a loose knot.

2 **Slide the knot up**
Carefully move the knot upwards until it reaches the needle.

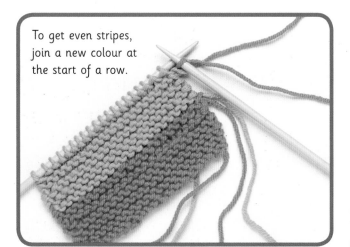

To get even stripes, join a new colour at the start of a row.

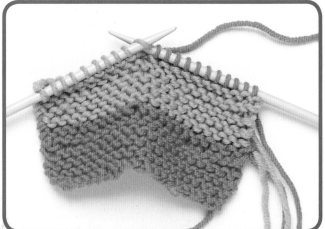

3 **Start knitting**
Now start knitting with the new colour.

4 **Knit to end of the row**
Knit as many rows as you like to make a stripe with your new colour.

Or try "self-striping".

My stripes were made with self-striping yarn.

Easy stripes
It's quicker to use self-striping yarns. Since they have so many colours, the stripes are created as you knit!

Add colour with stunning stripes.

My stripes were made with different coloured yarns.

Self-striping yarn comes in lots of **colour combinations**

These bags show two different sorts of stripes.

Purl stitch

This is another stitch to learn. Although you do it differently to knit stitch, it looks just the same!

yarn to the **front**

yarn **around** needle

 Put the needle in the stitch
Push the needle into the first stitch. The needle crosses in front of the left needle.

 Wrap yarn around needle
Holding yarn tightly, wrap it around the right needle from right to left.

Knit stitch is at the front.

The front is smooth with V-shaped stitches.

If you knit a row in knit stitch and the next row in purl, you make **stocking stitch.**

pull needle backwards

take off needle

3

Pull the needle through
Pull the right needle back and through taking yarn with it as your new loop.

4

Slip loop off left needle
Let the old loop slip off, your new loop will now be on your right needle.

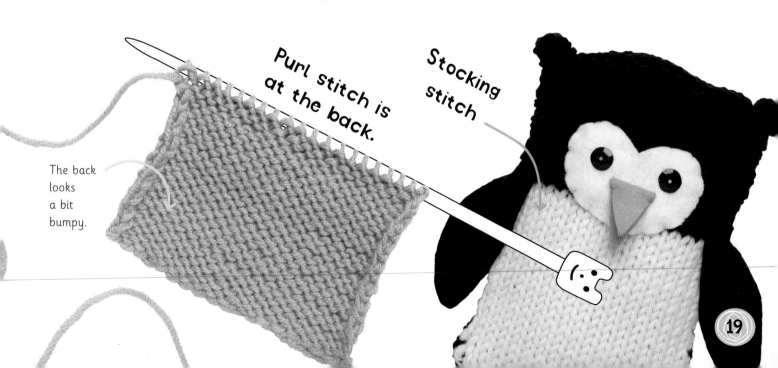

Purl stitch is at the back.

Stocking stitch

The back looks a bit bumpy.

You will need

double knit yarn • pair of 4mm
(No 6) knitting needles
• tapestry needle • crochet hook
• scissors • plastic fork

Fred's hat and scarf

This snuggly hat and scarf is finished off with a fluffy pom-pom and tassels.

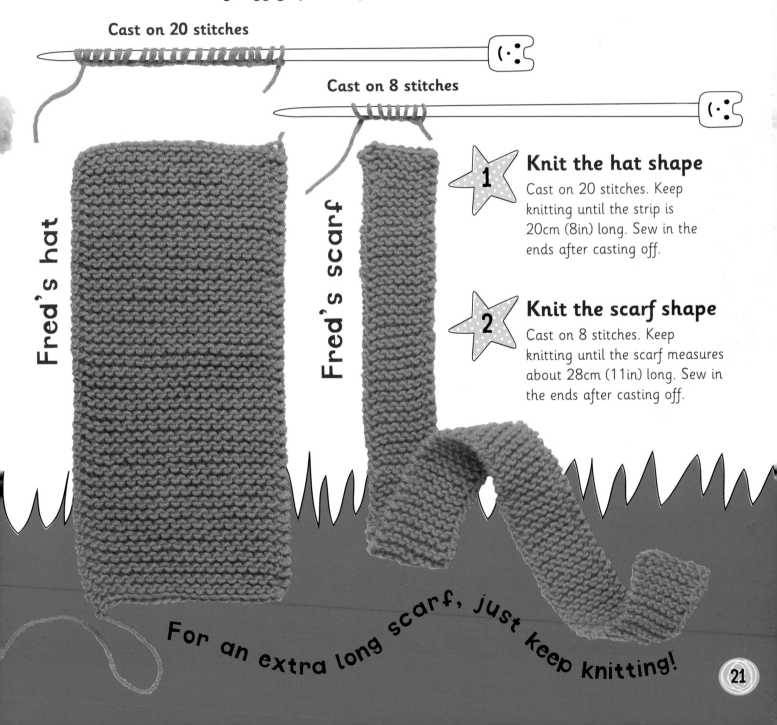

Cast on 20 stitches

Cast on 8 stitches

Fred's hat

Fred's scarf

1 Knit the hat shape

Cast on 20 stitches. Keep knitting until the strip is 20cm (8in) long. Sew in the ends after casting off.

2 Knit the scarf shape

Cast on 8 stitches. Keep knitting until the scarf measures about 28cm (11in) long. Sew in the ends after casting off.

For an extra long scarf, just keep knitting!

How to finish the hat

pull tight

Sew running stitch around one of the open edges.

 1 **Sew up one side**
Fold the hat rectangle in half then pin and sew up one side. Leave the two opposite sides open.

 2 **Close up the top**
Pull the yarn tight to close up the top of your hat and secure with one or two stitches.

How to make the scarf tassels

Use a crochet hook.

1 **Cut short pieces** of yarn and hook a loop through the end of the scarf.

2 **Pull the loop** right through with the crochet hook.

3 **Thread the ends** of the yarn through the loop. Pull tightly and trim with scissors.

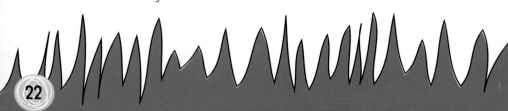

How to make a mini pom-pom

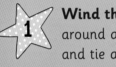

 1 **Wind the yarn** around a fork and tie a knot in the ends.

2 **Wrap the yarn** around and around. Thread the end through the prongs.

3 **Tie the two ends** of yarn together in a knot.

4 **With scissors,** snip the yarn at each side. Fluff up your pom-pom.

Sew a pom-pom onto the gathered end of the hat.

You can also sew on bells or felt shapes to our hats.

If you want to make a **smaller hat**, cast on 15 stitches and knit until the strip is 15cm (6in) long. For a **smaller scarf**, just cast on 6 stitches and knit as many rows as you like.

Big needles

If you like Fred's scarf and want one the same, just "big up" with fatter needles and chunky yarn.

Make yourself a scarf just like mine.

Knit the scarf

Cast on 12 stitches and knit until the scarf is 90cm (36in), or as long as you like. Cast off, then sew in any yarn ends.

See how much smaller the knitting is on Fred's scarf.

You will need

chunky yarn • pair of 12mm (US 17) needles • tapestry needle • scissors • crochet hook

If you use thin yarn and fat needles, you'll get loose, lacy knitting.

For fun, make **tassels in a different colour** to your scarf. Use as many colours as you like.

Make tassels in the same way as you did for Fred's scarf on page 22.

Brilliant bracelets

It's easy to knit these beautiful bracelets, and you can have fun decorating them with sparkly beads, pretty buttons, and ribbons.

Flat bracelets are the quickest and easiest to make. You can knit and decorate them in no time at all.

Rolled up bracelets

Sew your most beautiful **button** to the centre of the bracelet.

You will need
double knit yarn • pair of 4mm (No 6) knitting needles • tapestry needle • sewing needle • sewing thread • scissors • buttons • beads • ribbons

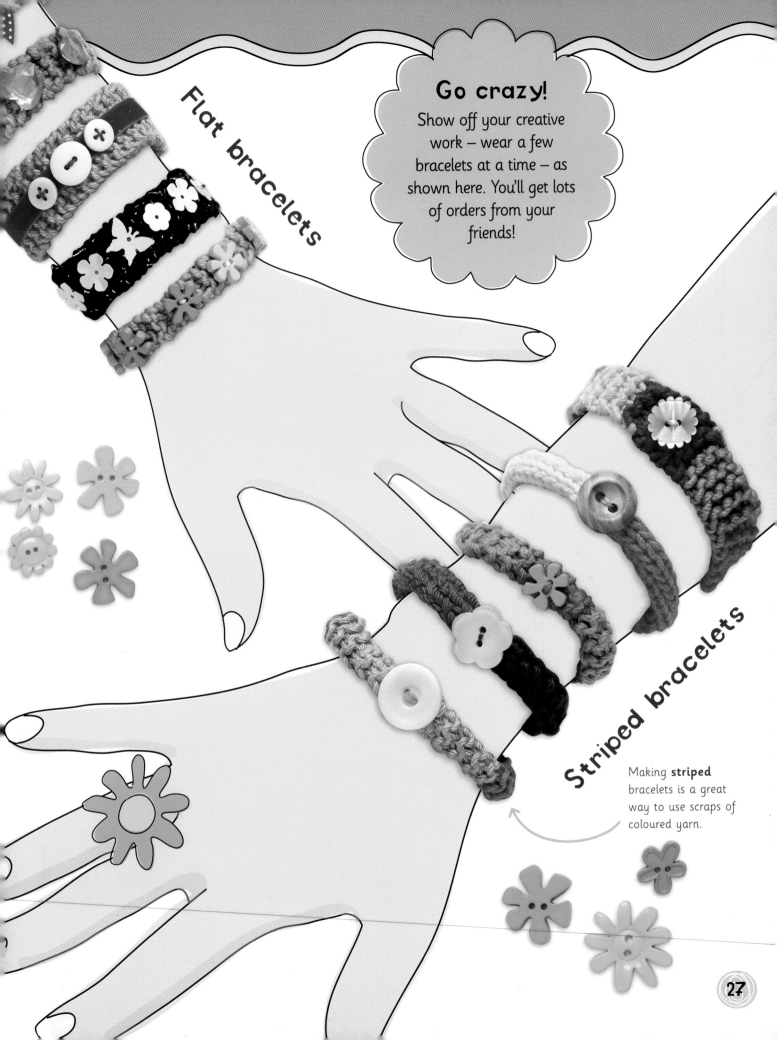

Flat bracelets

Go crazy!

Show off your creative work — wear a few bracelets at a time — as shown here. You'll get lots of orders from your friends!

Striped bracelets

Making **striped** bracelets is a great way to use scraps of coloured yarn.

How to make a rolled bracelet

Cast on 6 stitches

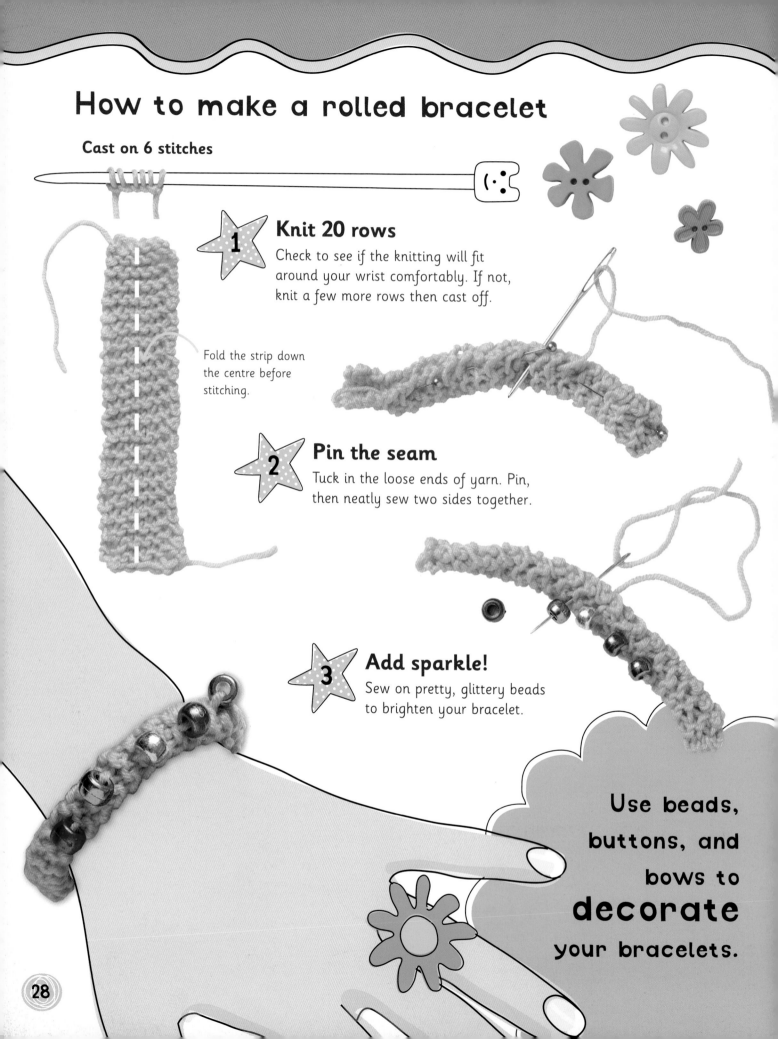

⭐1 Knit 20 rows
Check to see if the knitting will fit around your wrist comfortably. If not, knit a few more rows then cast off.

Fold the strip down the centre before stitching.

⭐2 Pin the seam
Tuck in the loose ends of yarn. Pin, then neatly sew two sides together.

⭐3 Add sparkle!
Sew on pretty, glittery beads to brighten your bracelet.

Use beads, buttons, and bows to **decorate** your bracelets.

Top tip

You can personalize bracelets to give as gifts by stitching your friends' names on them.

Different fastenings

Ribbon fastening

Cut two short lengths of fine ribbon. Sew a length to each end of your bracelet.

Stitch the ribbon firmly in place.

Use a loose end of yarn to **sew** the bracelet together.

Circle fastening

Stitch the two ends of the bracelet together.

Button and loop fastening

Sew a button to one end of your bracelet. At the other end, pull through a short length of yarn. Make a knot so a loop is formed. Check that it's big enough for your button to go through.

At one end, sew on a **button**.

Tie a **knot** in the ends of the yarn to make a loop.

Hoo wants to learn to knit?

Make a **stripy owl** friend in any colour — see page 16 to learn how to knit stripes.

You will need

double knit yarn • pair of 4mm (No 6) knitting needles • tapestry needle • thin paper • scissors • felt • soft-toy filling • needle and sewing thread • buttons

Night owls

These owls are a hoot! You can make them one colour or striped, and add felt faces and cute little scarves.

Cast on 5 stitches

Cast on 20 stitches

Let's start knitting!

Scarf

Body

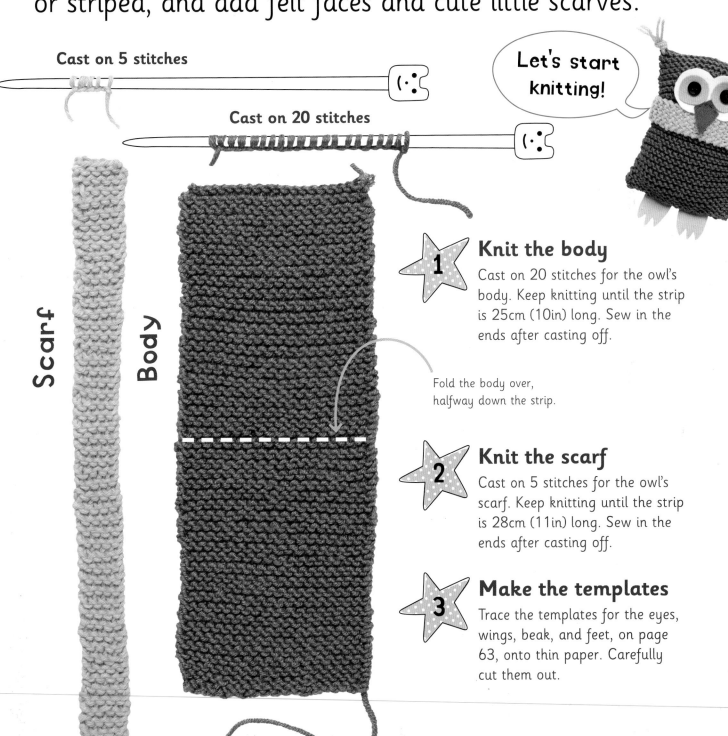

Fold the body over, halfway down the strip.

1 Knit the body

Cast on 20 stitches for the owl's body. Keep knitting until the strip is 25cm (10in) long. Sew in the ends after casting off.

2 Knit the scarf

Cast on 5 stitches for the owl's scarf. Keep knitting until the strip is 28cm (11in) long. Sew in the ends after casting off.

3 Make the templates

Trace the templates for the eyes, wings, beak, and feet, on page 63, onto thin paper. Carefully cut them out.

Make me in one of your favourite colours.

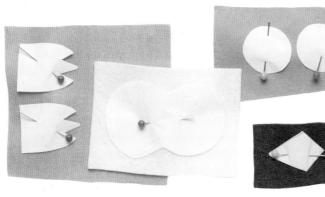

 4 Cut out the felt pieces
Pin the paper templates onto pieces of felt and carefully cut out the shapes.

 5 Sew up the body
With the same yarn that you used for the body, neatly sew around two edges. Then sew halfway along the third side.

Stitch the scarf here.

 8 Add the scarf
Put the scarf around your owl's neck. Pin it together, then stitch to hold it firmly in place.

 9 Attach the feet
Pin the feet to the back of your owl. Stitch in place.

Sew on the eyes and beak before you stitch them onto the body.

⭐6 Add the filling
Use soft-toy filling to stuff the body, pushing it into the corners. Then sew up the body to hold in the filling.

⭐7 Sew on the face
Sew through the buttons to attach the face to the body.

⭐10 Make tufty ears
Thread a needle with a short length of yarn. Push it through a top corner of the body. Snip the wool to release the needle. Tie in a knot and trim. Repeat for the other ear.

Trim my tufty ears to any length you like.

You will need

double knit yarn • pair of 4mm (No 6) knitting needles • tapestry needle • thin paper • felt • buttons • needle and sewing thread • soft-toy filling

Baa Baa white sheep, you are made of wool...

Baa! I love ewe, Mummy.

34

Knitted sheep

Once you get the hang of it, you can knit
a whole flock of sheep. If you count them,
mind you don't fall asleep!

Cast on 25 stitches.

Mummy sheep

 Knit the body
Cast on 25 stitches. Keep knitting
until the strip is 15cm (6in) long.
Sew in the ends after casting off.

 Make the templates
Trace the templates from page 63
onto thin paper. Carefully cut
them out.

Fold the body
over, halfway
down the strip.

Top tip
To make extra-soft
sheep, try using
fluffy white
yarn.

Love you
too.

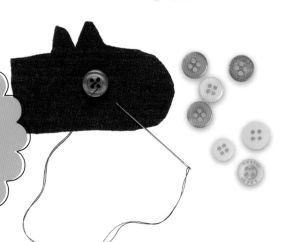

Top tip

For the eyes, find buttons in lots of colours, so your sheep all look different.

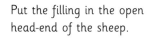

3 **Cut out the felt**

Pin your paper templates onto felt and carefully cut out the head and legs.

4 **Sew on the eyes**

For the eyes, sew a button to the middle of each side of the head.

Put the filling in the open head-end of the sheep.

7 **Add the filling**

Use soft-toy filling to stuff the body. Push it into the corners with a pencil or your finger.

8 **Sew the head in place**

Put the head in place, pin and then sew the edges together.

ewe, ram, and lamb.

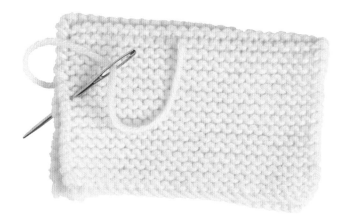

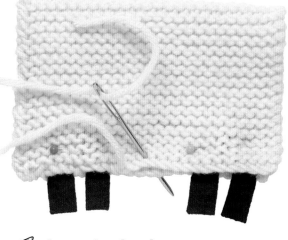

5 **Sew up the body**
Fold the sheep rectangle in half and sew along one short side.

6 **Attach the legs**
Pin the legs inside the long, open side then sew the edges together.

How are you, Woolly?

Make a ram
Cast on 25 stitches. Knit a 18cm (7in) strip. Then make in the same way as a mummy sheep.

Get the template for the horns on page 63.

Not too baaad!

Make a lamb
Cast on 15 stitches. Knit a 10cm (4in) strip. Make the lamb in the same way as a mummy sheep.

Sew funny faces on **your charms** or decorate with beads or buttons.

Add tufty ears to this owl charm.

Aren't I charming?

What big eyes I've got!

Bag charms

These cute little charms are perfect to customize your bags. They make good party bag gifts too.

You will need

double knit yarn · pair of 4mm (No 6) knitting needles · tapestry needle · needle and sewing thread · felt · buttons · soft-toy filling · ribbon

How to make a square charm

Cast on 20 stitches

Fold the **charm** halfway across

The side seam is now in the middle

⭐1 Knit the charm
Cast on 20 stitches. Keep knitting until the charm is 6cm (2½in) long. Cast off and sew in the ends.

⭐2 Sew the sides
Pin, then sew together one of the sides.

⭐3 Sew the top
Move the stitched seam to the middle, then sew up one of the open ends.

Top tip
For a lovely scent, add a pinch of fragrant lavender to your **soft-toy** filling.

Pin the **ribbon** then sew it onto the charm.

⭐4 Fill and sew
Push in soft-toy filling, then sew up the last open end to hold in the filling.

⭐5 Add a button
Decorate the charm by stitching on a button.

⭐6 Add a loop
Pin the ends of a ribbon to the back of the charm, and stitch it in place.

You will need

double knit yarn • pair of 4mm (No 6) knitting needles • tapestry needle • soft-toy filling • pencil • needle and sewing thread • buttons • ribbon • bells

Kitty cats

These cool cats are purr...fect. With their smart collars and bells, they're the cat's whiskers!

Cast on 18 stitches

Let's get knitting!

Cast on 8 stitches

kitten's body

Fold the body over halfway down.

kitten's tail

Knit the body

Cast on 18 stitches. Keep knitting until your knitting is 33cm (13in) long. Cast off then sew in the ends.

Knit the tail

Cast on 8 stitches. Knit until the tail measures 20cm (8in). Cast off then sew in the ends.

Fold the tail lengthwise down the centre.

You can make us in **any colour**, even blue or green!

3 Sew up two sides

Pin and sew two sides together. Then sew halfway up the third side, leaving a space to add the filling.

4 Add the filling

Use soft-toy filling to stuff the body – push it into the corners with a pencil. Then sew up the opening.

Attach the **whiskers** to the nose first.

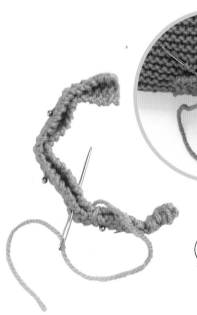

Top tip

For a curly tail, put a pipecleaner in the tail before sewing it up.

7 Sew on nose and whiskers

Sew on kitty cat's nose and whiskers, just below the eyes.

8 Make the tail

Sew the edges of the tail together. Stitch the tail onto the back of the kitten.

Make the ears

5 Pin and sew across each corner of the head to make the ears.

Top tip
Instead of buttons, you can glue beads or sequins onto your kitten.

Sew on the eyes

6 Sew on little buttons to make the eyes.

Pin the kitten's collar at the back before sewing it.

With this bell, I can't sneak up on anyone!

Add the collar

9 Push a piece of thread through a bell and tie it onto the collar. Wrap the collar around the kitten and sew to hold it firm.

Finger fun

Why not put on a show with these funny puppets? They're so quick to knit, you can make one for every finger!

Sew on yarn to make the hair.

Decorate **your puppets** with sequins, beads, buttons, and scraps of felt, yarn, or fabric.

Attach the felt eyes, sequins, and mouth with fabric glue.

You will need

double knit yarn • pair of 4mm (No 6) knitting needles • tapestry needle • needle and sewing thread • felt • buttons • sequins

How to make a finger puppet

Cast on 15 stitches

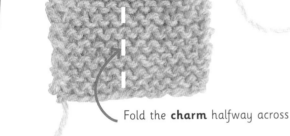

Fold the **charm** halfway across

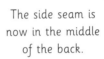

The side seam is now in the middle of the back.

1 Knit the body
Cast on 20 stitches. Keep knitting until the body is 6cm (2½in) long. Cast off and sew in the ends.

2 Sew the sides
Pin, then stitch together one of the sides.

3 Sew the top
Move the stitched seam to the middle, then sew one of the open ends.

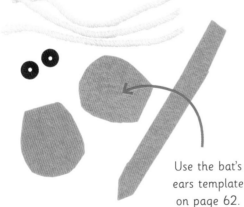

Use the bat's ears template on page 62.

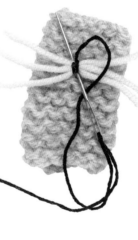

Top tip

If you want bigger **finger puppets**, just use larger knitting needles.

4 Make the extras
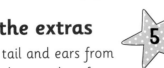

Cut out a tail and ears from felt, using the template for the bat's ears. Cut three short lengths of yarn for the whiskers.

5 Sew on the whiskers

Use black sewing thread to sew on the whiskers, so the thread looks like a nose.

6 Sew on the eyes and ears
Sew on sequins for the eyes, and sew the ears and tail onto the body.

Want to go out flying tonight?

Bat-tastic bats

With their cute fangs and googly eyes, these batty bats are fun to make. Hang a few up together for a great bat-mobile.

You will need

double knit yarn • pair of 4mm (No 6) knitting needles • tapestry needle • thin paper • felt • needle and sewing thread • googly eyes • fabric glue • soft-toy filling

46

family of lovable little acro-bats!

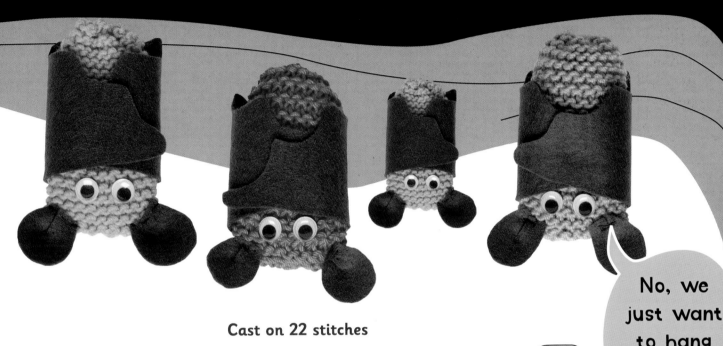

Cast on 22 stitches

No, we just want to hang around.

⭐ 1   Knit the bat's body

Cast on 22 stitches. Keep knitting until the strip is 9cm (3½in) long. Cast off then sew in the ends.

⭐ 2   Make the templates

Trace the templates for the wings and ears on page 62 onto thin paper. Carefully cut them out.

Fold the body down the centre.

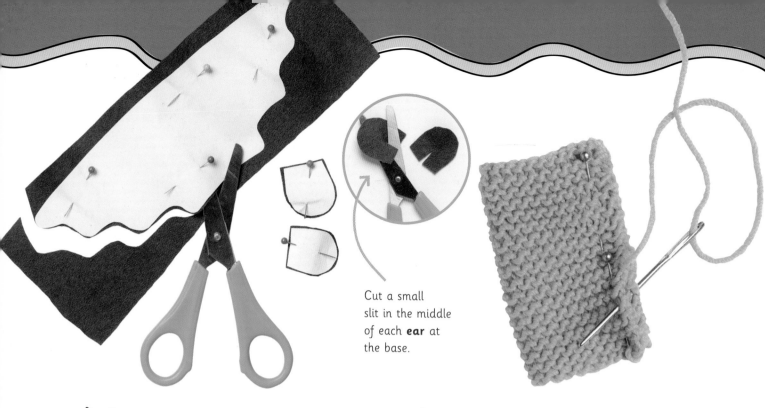

Cut a small slit in the middle of each **ear** at the base.

3

Cut out the felt pieces

Pin the paper templates onto pieces of felt and carefully cut out the shapes.

4

Sew up the body

Pin the long sides, then neatly sew them together.

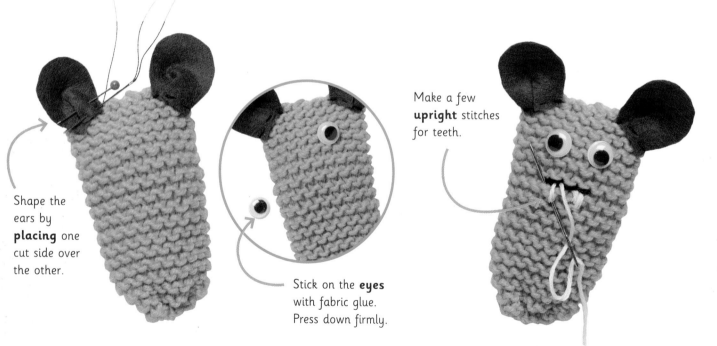

Shape the ears by **placing** one cut side over the other.

Stick on the **eyes** with fabric glue. Press down firmly.

Make a few **upright** stitches for teeth.

7

Sew on the ears

Pin the ears to each side at the top of the body then sew them on.

8

Stitch on mouth and teeth

Sew stitches in black thread for the mouth. Sew on fangs using white thread.

Move the sewn edges to the centre, at the back of the bat's body.

Pull tight!

5 **Add the filling**
Pin and sew one of the short sides together. Stuff with soft-toy filling, pushing it into the corners.

6 **Close up**
Sew running stitch along the open end. Pull the thread tight and secure with a stitch.

Let's go for a bite to eat!

9 **Sew on the wings**
Pin the wings to the centre of the bat's back. Sew onto the bat with running stitch.

Top tip
Stitch thread to your bat's head, so you can hang it up.

knitted straps

bags with long straps

short handles

Knitted handles

Knit the handles of your bags as **thick or thin**, and as **long or short** as you want. You can use ribbon, too.

Stripes

To learn how to make **stripes**, see pages 15 and 16.

Bag bonanza

Although they look amazing, these bags are so **easy** to make, and you can pretty them up any way you like.

Decorate!
Rows of braid and ribbons, and buttons of different shapes and sizes, will make your bags look fabulous.

bags with ribbon straps

bags with sparkly sequins

Decorate with buttons, pom-poms, ribbon, and sequins.

You will need

double knit yarn • pair of 4mm (No 6) knitting needles • tapestry needle • needle and sewing thread • ribbon • sequin ribbon • button

Fold the knitting over, halfway down the strip.

Cast on 25 stitches

1 Knit the bag

Cast on 25 stitches. Keep knitting until the strip is 22cm (9in) long. Cast off then sew in the ends.

Make a **loop** on the back of the bag.

3 Sew on a button

On the front of the bag, sew on a button. Trim the ends of the thread neatly.

4 Make a button loop

Using a double thickness of thread, sew a loop. Knot the ends together to hold it in place.

More brilliant bag ideas...

Drawstring bag

Make a bag as shown, then thread ribbon or cord about 2.5cm (1in) from the top. Tie a knot in the ends. Pull the ribbon tight to close the bag.

Add a beautiful button that matches the **drawstring**.

2 ## Sew up two sides

Pin the sides, then neatly sew them together.

Sew the ends of the ribbon **handle** to the inside of the bag.

Sew rows of **sequin ribbon** around the bag with running stitch.

Useful pouch

This pouch can be used for a phone, for pencils, or even as a sleeping bag for your small soft toys. Cast on 15 stitches, then knit a strip 30cm (12in) long. Cast off then sew in the ends. Leave a flap at the top, then sew up the sides.

 ## Now decorate!

Sew ribbon all around the bag to decorate. Then sew on a length of ribbon to make the handle.

Decorate this cool mobile phone case with a **funny face**. Sew on felt teeth, and add buttons for eyes.

You will need

double knit yarn • pair of 4mm (no 6) knitting needles • felt • tapestry needle • thin paper • soft-toy filling • needle and sewing thread • fabric glue • sequins

Top tip

For the fish, cut out fish shapes in felt, and sew or glue on a bead for each eye.

Gone fishing. What a catch!

Percy penguin

You'll need two colours of yarn to make this sweet little penguin. He's so cool!

Cast on 18 stitches in black.

1 **Knit the body**

Cast on 18 stitches in black yarn. Keep knitting until your knitting is 20cm (8in) long. Change to white yarn and knit 9cm (3½in) in stocking stitch (alternate rows of knit and purl).

2 **Make the templates**

Trace the templates from page 63 onto thin paper. Carefully cut them out.

Knit stitch

Fold the body over halfway down the strip.

Stocking stitch

If you don't want to use stocking stitch just make me all in **knit stitch**.

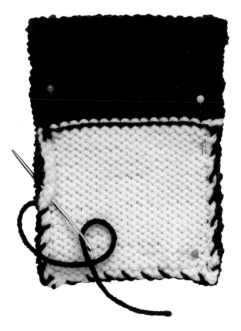

3 Cut out the felt pieces

Pin your paper templates onto felt and carefully cut out the flippers, feet, and beak.

4 Sew up the body

With right sides together, fold the body in half. Sew around the edges, leaving a gap at the side of the head for the filling. Turn the body right side out.

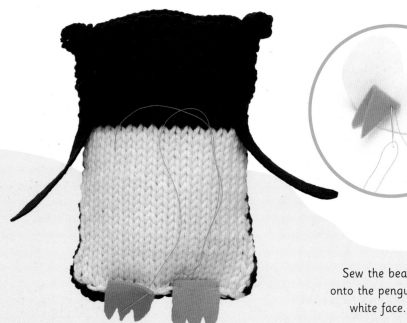

Sew the beak onto the penguin's white face.

7 Attach the feet

Sew the feet onto the front of Percy penguin's body.

8 Sew on the face

Sew around the face to hold it in place.

Now you can see the **right side** with black knit stitch and white stocking stitch

Sew up each corner of the head to make the ears.

Hey wait for me!

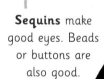

5 Stuff with the filling

Push soft-toy filling into the body with a pencil. Sew up the gap to hold the filling in place.

6 Add the flippers

Sew a flipper onto each side of the body.

Sequins make good eyes. Beads or buttons are also good.

Glue

Use fabric glue to stick on the eyes. It's quite sticky and fiddly, so ask an adult to help you.

9 Add the eyes

Use a little glue to stick down the eyes.

Wheee... go with the floe!

Sally the snake

This stripy snake is a real charmer. She's made with a special self-striping yarn, but you can use separate colours if you like.

Cast on 30 stitches

You will need

double knit self-striping yarn
• pair of 4mm (No 6) knitting
needles • tapestry needle
• thin paper • soft-toy filling
• felt • buttons • needle and
sewing thread

The self-striping yarn
creates irregular
stripes that are perfect
for Sally's body.

**Self- striping
yarn** works like
magic! Just keep
knitting and see how
the colours change all
by themselves.

Make Sally's body as long as you like.

1 ### Knit the body
Cast on 30 stitches. Keep
knitting until your knitting
is about 74cm (29in) long.

2 ### Make the templates
Trace the tongue and eye templates
from page 62 onto thin paper.
Carefully cut them out.

Top tip

To make a rattlesnake, pop a bell inside the tail end of your snake.

⭐ **3**

Close up the tail end

Sew running stitch around one short edge. Pull the yarn tight and secure with a stitch.

Jingle
Jangle

Stuff Sally as evenly as you

Pull the thread tight.

⭐ **6**

Close up

Sew running stitch around the edge of the head. Pull the thread tight and secure with a stitch.

⭐ **7**

Cut out the felt pieces

Pin your paper templates onto felt and carefully cut out two eyes and a tongue.

⭐ **8**

Sew on the eyes

Stitch one button and felt circle onto each side of Sally's head.

⭐ 4 Sew up the body
Sew up part of the body, then stuff it. Repeat all the way up the body.

⭐ 5 Stuff the head
Finally, stuff Sally's head.

can so she looks smooth.

Stitch Sally in a contrasting colour.

This colourful snake is made from **four colours of yarn**. He looks different – but he's just as good-looking as Sally.

⭐ 9 Sew on the tongue
Stitch the forked tongue to the front of her head.

Hello, my name is Bill. I'm a banded snake.

Templates

Use these handy templates to cut out the felt shapes you'll need to make lots of the projects in this book.

How to make a template

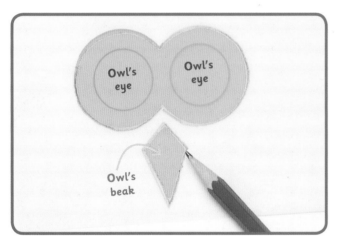

> Ask an **adult to help you cut** out the templates.

1 Draw the templates
Place thin paper over the templates shown here. Then carefully trace them.

2 Cut out the templates
Carefully cut around the shapes then follow the instructions for the project.

Bat from page 46

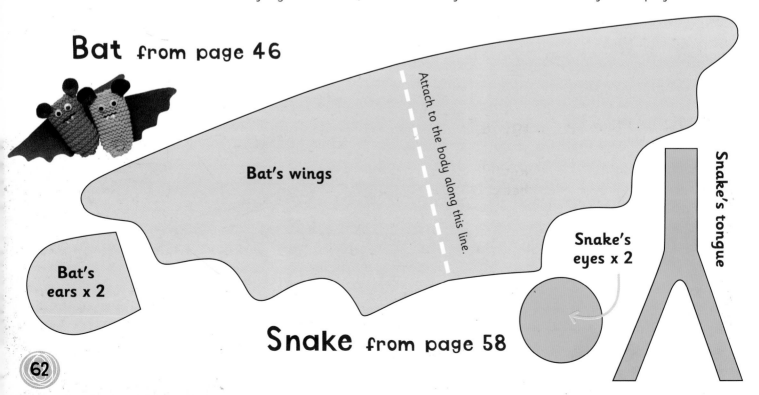

Bat's wings

Attach to the body along this line.

Bat's ears x 2

Snake's tongue

Snake's eyes x 2

Snake from page 58

Sheep from page 34

Adult sheep's legs

Adult sheep's head

Lamb's head

Lamb's legs

Ram's horns

Owl from page 30

Owl's face

Owl's eye

Owl's eye

Owl's feet x 2

Owl's beak

Owl's wings x 2

Draw around the templates carefully.

Penguin from page 54

Penguin's face

Penguin's beak

fold

Penguin's feet x 2

Penguin's flippers x 2

Index

Acknowledgements

With thanks to Kathryn Meeker, Wendy Horobin, and Toby Mann for proofreading.

With special thanks to model Eleanor Moore-Smith; Hannah Moore for creating the projects; and Sandra Moore for knitting and making them.

And when you've finished don't forget to tidy up!